Tai Chi FOR KIDS

jose**figueroa**
stephan**berwick**

Tuttle Publishing
Tokyo • Rutland, Vermont • Singapore

First published in the United States in 2005 by
Tuttle Publishing, an imprint of Periplus Editions (HK) Ltd.,
with editorial offices at 364 Innovation Drive,
North Clarendon, Vermont 05759.

Library of Congress Control Number: 2005920628

ISBN 0-8048-3563-2

IMPORTANT NOTE TO READERS:
Training in the martial arts involves physical exertion,
movements, and actions that can cause injury to you or others.
Because the physical activities in this book may be too strenuous
for some readers, you should check with a physician before you
start your training. If you are ever in doubt about how to
proceed or about whether a practice is safe for you, consult with
a martial arts professional before proceeding.

DISTRIBUTED BY

North America, Latin America, and Europe
Tuttle Publishing
364 Innovation Drive
North Clarendon, VT 05759-9436
Tel: (802) 773-8930
Fax: (802) 773-6993
info@tuttlepublishing.com
www.tuttlepublishing.com

Japan
Tuttle Publishing
Yaekari Building, 3rd Floor
5-4-12 Ōsaki
Shinagawa-ku
Tokyo 141 0032
Tel: (03) 5437-0171
Fax: (03) 5437-0755
tuttle-sales@gol.com

Asia Pacific
Berkeley Books Pte. Ltd.
130 Joo Seng Road
#06-01/03 Olivine Building
Singapore 368357
Tel: (65) 6280-1330
Fax: (65) 6280-6290
inquiries@periplus.com.sg
www.periplus.com

First edition
08 07 06 05   10 9 8 7 6 5 4 3 2 1
Printed in Malaysia

Illustrations by Stephanie Tok
Design by Kathryn Sky-Peck

CONTENTS

One

WHAT IS TAI CHI?

Tai Chi is a Chinese martial art that was created about 400 years ago. It was originally created for combat, but many people practice Tai Chi to improve their health, calm their mind, and better their life.

PHILOSOPHY

Tai Chi is based on the notion that all things have a way of balancing themselves through the laws of yin and yang. Yin and yang are opposites, and nothing exists without its opposite—up and down, left and right, front and back, hard and soft, fast and slow.

Yin and yang are complex ideas. You may not understand them completely right at the beginning, but these important terms will become clearer to you as you practice Tai Chi. Yang is an active, giving energy. People also think of it as the light in the duo light/dark or the male in male/female. Yin is a passive, receiving energy. It is the dark in light/dark and the female in male/female. It is important to understand that each person has both yin and yang energy and yin and yang aspects. The flow of energy in a person's body is called qi. This energy is constantly changing—moving in and out of balance, ebbing and flowing. Like yin and yang, qi is something you will learn to understand better the longer you practice Tai Chi. Tai Chi balances your internal energy, your yin and yang.

Tai Chi's exercises are made up of a series of complicated movements that embody the opposition of yin and yang. When you practice Tai Chi correctly, you will experience both effort and tranquility, agility and power.

Tai Chi provides the benefits of exercise without the dangers of high-impact sports. It is famous for building energy and helping you recover from injuries. It can strengthen your joints so that you are less prone to injury. It can also increase the level of oxygen in your blood (which helps your athletic performance) without the stress of other training methods.

Tai Chi will help you get your body and mind working together as one. Your breathing will improve. You'll have better balance (because of the motor skills you practice), better emotional health (from the peace and serenity you'll find in practicing the slow, measured movements), and heightened senses (from your concentration on the movements), and you'll be able to deal with pain better (through deep breathing and better body alignment).

Along with these mental and physical benefits, Tai Chi is also a great method of self-defense. It uses the laws of physics and the principles of circular movement to help you balance the forces within you against the forces coming from an opponent.

In Tai Chi, you deflect, absorb, and redirect forces brought against you. This makes it possible for you to defend yourself against an opponent with superior strength. In fact, the stronger your opponent, the more energy you have available in a countermove.

Tai Chi also emphasizes evasive techniques—ways to skillfully avoid attacks—as a healthy alternative to combat in our often-confrontational world.

Tai Chi is one of the best things you can do for your body. It requires minimal physical effort and can help you achieve a relaxed, calm mind. Do you want to jump higher, run faster, and lift heavier objects? Tai Chi will help you develop those skills in a safe, long-lasting way.

Tai Chi does all this, plus it looks cool!

Yin, Yang and Communication

Yin and yang represent complementary opposites. In the Tai Chi class, there are two possible forms of communication—yin and yang. If the teacher is speaking, he or she is yang. If you were speaking at the same time, then you would also be yang. Like two palms pressing against each other with equal strength, this can lead to a conflict—in any case, it makes it difficult to learn anything! If one person becomes yin and listens, you can have a conversation. In class, the teacher usually takes a yang role, while the students should adopt a yin approach to learning.

HISTORY AND STYLES

In order to get a better understanding of Tai Chi, let's take a quick look at its history.

Tai Chi, or Tai Chi Chuan, translates literally as "Grand Ultimate Fist." Tai Chi started as a style of Chinese boxing. It was created in the late Ming dynasty (1600s) by the respected general, Chen Wangting, who combined Chinese medicine, the energy principles of qi, controlled breathing, and the theory of yin and yang with boxing methods developed by the famous general Qi Jiguang. The original Chen boxing style featured a balance of fast and slow—and hard and soft—movements that were both excellent for self-defense and promoted good health.

Chen Wangting's family kept Tai Chi secret for several centuries. It seems likely that the Chen family form of Tai Chi is the original source for all the other styles (such as the very popular Yang style) that have developed since then. It's different from the others because it includes both soft and hard movements. Chen style is also unique in its use of "coiling" or "twining" (also known as "silk reeling") movements, or *chan szu jing*, that create enormous power.

While there are many styles of Tai Chi, there are also different styles of Chen Tai Chi. The most enduring version was developed by Chen Changxing and is known today as the Lao Jia or "Old Frame." The Lao Jia style exhibits the long, flowing movements characteristic of Northern Chinese boxing.

6

Chen Fake, a Chen family grandmaster and genius from the middle of the last century, created the Xin Jia or "New Frame" version of the Lao Jia forms. While very popular today, Xin Jia is considered more difficult to learn because it uses a lot of twining movements.

A third form of Chen Tai Chi, Xiao Jia or "Small Frame" style, features more compact movements and is gaining in popularity.

Regardless of style, each version of Chen style sticks to the original concepts of chan szu jing, the silk reeling energy.

TAI CHI TODAY

It may look easy at first, or maybe not as exciting as some other sports, but learning Tai Chi's slow, measured movements can be both challenging and inspiring. The mental and physical benefits of Tai Chi greatly outweigh the difficulties.

This book presents Tai Chi basics, such as stances and footwork, introduces Tai Chi training, and provides fun solo and partner Tai Chi exercises. We hope that you will enjoy learning about Tai Chi and applying the cooperative techniques it promotes.

Words to Know

Tai Chi—Grand Ultimate, (pronounced "tie chee")

Tai Chi Chuan—Grand Ultimate Fist, (pronounced "tie chee chwan")

Yin & Yang—The opposites of all things, dark/light, light/heavy, left/right, slow/fast, empty/full.

Qi—Life force, the internal energy that fuels all living things. (pronounced "jee")

Chen Wangting—The Ming dynasty (late 1600s) founder of Tai Chi.

Chan szu jing— Silk reeling energy, (pronounced "chaan zhu jing")

Zhang zhuang—Standing with intent and fullness.

Tui shou—Push hands, (pronounced "twee shou")

two

GETTING READY

In this chapter we'll discuss how you can prepare yourself for a Tai Chi class. Not only should you know what to wear, but it's also important to understand the attitude and etiquette you need to bring to each class.

WHAT YOU SHOULD WEAR

What you wear to class depends on the school you go to, so it's important to ask your teacher what he or she prefers the students to wear. Some teachers take a more traditional approach: in these cases the student would wear a designated uniform. Other teachers are a bit more relaxed about uniforms but require a school T-shirt that might be used as a class uniform. Most teachers recommend some kind of cotton outfit.

Regardless of dress code, you should wear clothing that is comfortable and loose-fitting because it is important that your clothing does not get in the way of your movement. The clothing you wear to Tai Chi class should be no different from most exercise clothing, which allows the body to move freely. Here are some suggestions.

Top

The top should not be too tight. It should be a relaxed fitting shirt that allows for a full range of motion. A traditional Chinese martial arts top can be worn, but sweatshirts and T-shirts are fine as well. Cotton fabrics are usually a good choice because they absorb moisture. Rayon-cotton blend fabrics also have a nice, smooth feel.

Bottoms

Your bottoms should be made of a similar cotton or cotton-rayon blend. They can be long pants or even shorts. They should fit nicely at your waist and should have enough room in the thigh, hip, and groin areas for easy movement. These bottoms should allow space for spreading your legs apart, because this type of movement is necessary for Tai Chi.

Undergarments

For boys, snug-fitting underwear will provide proper support. Any athletic sports wear is suitable for girls, but a good sports bra or snug T-shirt is also a good choice.

Shoes

Shoes should be low-cut. Indoor soccer sneakers, table tennis sneakers, or even skateboard shoes are recommended. These types of shoes usually have flat soles and provide the right traction; their light weight also makes them ideal for Tai Chi practice. Flat-soled sneakers provide more stability for the constant foot pivoting and stomping required by Chen Tai Chi.

Basketball or running shoes have too much insole padding and a curved exterior rubber heel that prevents the natural feel your feet need when practicing. Other martial arts shoes, such as kung fu shoes, are flat-soled but probably do not have enough arch support for the foot stomping executed in Chen Tai Chi.

RULES AND ETIQUETTE

Rules and etiquette vary from teacher to teacher. But there is one constant: you must always show respect for your teacher and classmates. Here are a few rules of etiquette for proper behavior in class.

How to Act toward the Teacher

Teachers are given the highest level of respect in any martial arts school. They are usually greeted by their students with a salute. You perform this salute by placing your left palm (open and flat) over your right clenched fist and then bowing by leaning slightly forward.

Paying attention to your teacher's instructions is important, because Tai Chi can be very complex and has many small

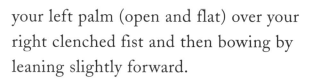

details hidden within the movements. Above all, you should always demonstrate a high level of respect for your teacher—expressing your appreciation for the privilege of learning this specialized art.

How to Act toward One Another

You should treat other students in your class as you like to be treated yourself. A great deal of camaraderie—a strong sense of brotherhood and sisterhood—develops in most martial arts schools. There is also a strong sense of hierarchy that reflects your ability and commitment. Class members may be identified as older brother, younger brother, sister, uncle, and so on. Your teacher determines your rank, based on

When you salute, you are showing more than respect for your teacher and Tai Chi. The fist represents power and strength, while the open palm represents humility and respect. It is important to have both of these qualities at all times.

your hard work, ability, and persistence. A second-year student, for example, will usually be senior to someone with only one year of training experience. Unlike Karate, which uses colored belts to illustrate hierarchy, Tai Chi schools don't have formal symbols or insignia. Those chosen, however, share a strong bond of profound respect for their teacher, one another, and their art.

three

THE TAI CHI CLASS

Traditional Tai Chi schools are centered on a main training hall. This room should be wide—as most Tai Chi forms travel from right to left. There should be plenty of room to move in all directions. The centerpiece of the main training hall is usually an area devoted to a display of the school's teaching lineage. Here students can show respect to the ancestors of their chosen Tai Chi style. The formal arrangement of the classroom should serve as a constant reminder that you should demonstrate respect for the room and your teacher when you enter.

WHAT HAPPENS IN A TYPICAL CLASS

Classes usually start with standing practice (*zhang zhuang*, see page 22). These are stationary exercises in which you hold a specific posture for an extended period of time. They can help you develop proper body posture, leg strength, and the upper body relaxation necessary to perform Tai Chi movements. They both set the tone for the whole class and help you focus on your practice. They also sharpen your mental concentration, develop your experience of qi (internal energy), and stimulate the circulation of this energy. Zhang zhuang is probably the most important part of your training, because it builds the foundation for strength as well as focus.

After standing practice, most classes move into warm-ups and stretching (see page 13).

The more complicated "silk reeling" or chan szu jing exercises (see page 29) would be the last step in a warm-up sequence. These are motor skill sequences taken from the traditional choreographed forms. You'll also practice the basic movements of Tai Chi. After these exercises are completed, most classes will practice forms (or sequences), followed by partner exercises or sparring such as *tui shou* (push hands).

When your class ends, it is customary to line up with your classmates facing your teacher. You will repeat the salute you learned a few pages ago—place your right fist against your left palm and bow.

> The beauty of Tai Chi is that each person develops at his or her own pace. There is no rush to learn quickly; you should simply follow your own path and schedule. If you try your best, you will get the desired result.

HOW TO GET THE MOST OUT OF EACH CLASS

Though your teacher will play a crucial role in your development of Tai Chi, it is also important that you take responsibility for yourself and your own learning. Here are some important things to remember that will help your Tai Chi.

Stay Safe

The safety aspects of Tai Chi are part of the actual movements—if you are respectful of the movements and your fellow classmates, you shouldn't get hurt. Because you practice sequences at slow speeds—focusing on the accuracy of your movements—the risk of injury is relatively low. Sparring is also relatively safe—the objective is to unbalance your opponent, rather than strike him or her. You'll learn how to fall safely to the ground—along with controlling your partner—as part of the push hands exercise. Make sure to keep the practice area clear of objects that might get in the way or injure someone.

Tai Chi stresses nonconfrontational behavior. Bruce Lee said, "If you don't get hit, you don't have a reason to hit." This is important to remember as you learn Tai Chi.

Start Small

As you begin your journey toward learning Tai Chi, remember that you are traveling without knowing where you are going. Until you've practiced the movements many times, it is impossible to know how it feels to do

The Main Elements of a Tai Chi Class

1. Zhang zhuang

2. Warm-ups and stretching

3. Chan szu jing

4. Basic Tai Chi movements

5. Form or sequence practice

6. Partner exercises

them correctly. Take the time to take small steps. As you feel your body getting stronger, slowly set your goals higher, and make your movements bold and more expressive.

Stick to Your Routine

Try not to change around too much. Once you've learned something, practice it daily in a routine that stays the same. You can try variations of Tai Chi games so you don't get bored, but always give time to the same routine—so that you can see and feel the improvement as you progress.

Don't Overdo It

As always, listen to your body when you learn something new. Pay careful attention to the way your body is reacting. Sometimes we get carried away with practice, and don't pay attention to the way our bodies feel. Make an effort to notice when something doesn't feel natural or hurts. It could mean that your body is being overworked or that you're practicing incorrectly. If this happens, you should back off. You won't be able to practice if you're hurt, and you won't improve if you can't practice.

Be Aware of Your Body

Your body has natural ranges of motion. When you go beyond them, your body will feel pain. Be careful not to bend so far that you can't move into another position without straining. If you can't move comfortably, you've probably gone too far.

Be Patient

Don't try to advance too quickly. Tai Chi requires much more patience than other martial arts, because it's so complicated. You have to develop many different skills slowly—as you increase in knowledge and understanding. The journey is a long one, but think of it as a pleasant cruise, because when you get to where you're going, the parts that seem most difficult will seem clear, easy, and fun!

Try Your Best

The beauty of Tai Chi is that everyone develops at their own pace. Because the forms are practiced slowly, you can track the gradual progress you make. Tai Chi fosters progressive development: as you learn the postures, your body becomes stronger. There is no rush to learn quickly; you should simply follow your own path and schedule. If you try your best, you will get the desired result. Growth in Tai Chi is personal. Progress is measured by perseverance and patience, both of which you'll develop as you learn the basics of Tai Chi.

Have Fun

Don't forget to laugh at yourself when you make mistakes. Making mistakes is part of learning, and it's important to find the humor in why you couldn't stand on one leg longer than your friend. If you're competing with each other, make sure it's a cooperative game rather than being about winning. Push hands practice, for example, is about cooperation, not about who gets defeated. As you get better, you'll see that a good match is one where both you and your partner go for a long time without stopping! So have fun!

four
WARMING UP

You should start every Tai Chi class with warm-ups. Getting your body ready will help you to avoid injuries. And warming up gets you mentally prepared, which will help you get the most out of your class.

WARM-UPS

These simple warm-ups will get your body moving and ready for stretching. Warming-up your body before doing any stretching will help you avoid injuries—it's better for your muscles if you're at least breaking a sweat. Any form of body movement can be used, but here are a few exercises you can try.

KNEE ROTATION—FEET APART

You start this exercise by opening your legs shoulders' width apart and placing your hands directly under your knees. While supporting your knees with your hands, begin to circle both knees in opposite directions, first moving them out to in and then in to out. Repeat this exercise 8–12 times.

Knee rotation—feet apart

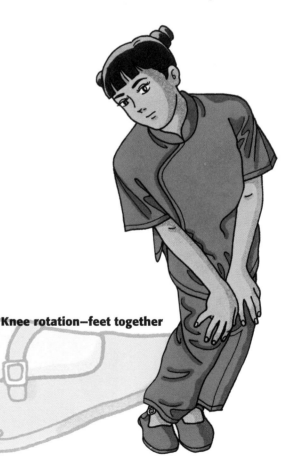

Knee rotation—feet together

KNEE ROTATION–FEET TOGETHER

Here you repeat the same hand placement as for the feet apart knee rotation, only now both knees circle to the right—and then to the left—at the same time.

SIMULTANEOUS WRIST AND ANKLE ROTATION

Place the toes of your right foot on the floor to the side of your body while lacing the fingers of both hands together. Rotate your clasped hands while also rotating your ankle, changing the direction of the rotations after 8–10 repetitions.

Simultaneous wrist and ankle rotation

TRUNK TURNS

Start with your feet shoulders' width apart. Relax your arms to the sides of your body. Twist your waist from left to right while allowing your arms to freely swing across your chest area. In this version of the exercise, your feet are facing forward and are firmly planted on the ground.

Trunk turns

In the second version of the exercise, shift your weight from one leg to the other as you lift the toes of each foot off the floor, pivoting on your heel, one side at a time. Continue with the same arm movement as you twist your trunk.

SHOULDER SLAPS

Still with your feet shoulders' width apart, swing your arms freely across your chest as if you were hugging yourself, then swing them back as far as you can.

WRIST COILING

With your legs shoulders' width apart, place the back of your right wrist on top of your right hip and circle your hand toward your navel, completely twisting your hand around at the wrist. Repeat with the other hand. Then, twist your hands forward, then backward for 8–10 repetitions with each hand. Try to move your hips and elbows in the same direction of your wrist as it rotates, with your knees bent.

Shoulder slaps

Back slaps

15

BACK SLAPS

Swing your arms up and over your shoulders, slapping the backs of your shoulders with your fingers. Then, swing your arms back down and behind you. Swing them back to the front at the end of every swing.

Wrist coiling

BREATHING WARM-UPS

These breathing warm-ups will help to focus your mind for Tai Chi practice. They'll also help to generate the internal energy, or qi, you need for the Tai Chi movements.

PALMS ON BELLY

Try this simple technique to make sure that you're breathing fully and deeply. Place both palms with the fingers spread widely on your lower abdomen. Place your tongue on the roof of your mouth, and inhale and

Palms on belly

exhale through your nose. As you inhale try to push your hands and fingers apart with each inhalation. When you exhale, close your fingers, pushing the air out. Your hand movements will imitate the inflating and deflating a balloon. You should do this in the zhang zhuang standing position (see page 22; it can also be practiced lying down or seated.

DIAPHRAGM BREATHING

Once you feel comfortable with the first breathing exercise, try it without your hands on your belly. Instead, imagine that your hands are still resting on your lower abdomen. Practice pushing the belly out and in. This can be done with your hands hanging at your sides.

STRETCHES

Now that your body is fully warmed up, you can begin your stretches. It's important to remember never to stretch past your limit. Listen to your body. If you're uncomfortable, adjust to a more comfortable position. Perform the following stretching exercises in the order they're listed in, because each exercise is progressively harder.

SQUAT STRETCH

Stand with your feet shoulders' width apart. Slowly sink into a sitting position. Your feet

Squat stretch

should be flat on the ground from toe to heel. Your toes should point somewhat outward. You can place your hands on the floor directly in front of you for balance. Hold this position for 30 seconds, and then rise slowly, using your hands to push off the floor, if necessary.

HAMSTRING ROWS

Stand with your legs about three feet apart. Fold your arms across each other, and extend your elbows reaching down in front of your body. Allow your arms to slide down toward your knees, coming as close to your shins as possible, and then slowly bounce up to repeat. This is similar to rowing a boat. You should bring your arms down and up in a circular fashion, going from out to in and then from in to out. Slowly "row" at least five times.

Hamstring rows

SLIDE STRETCH

Start from a standing position. Shift your weight to your right leg and sink down as far as you can, extending your left leg out to your side. Place both hands in front of your body, leaning slightly forward. Your body weight should be supported equally on both arms. Gently shift your stance to the left leg as you extend the right leg to the other side. Hold the posture for 20 seconds, then switch to your other leg.

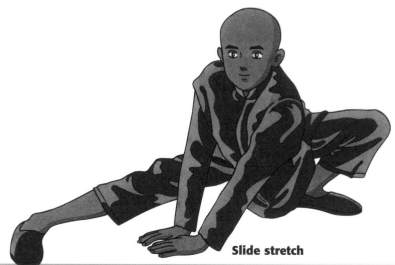

Slide stretch

HEAD TO KNEE

Stand with your legs about three feet apart. Reach toward your right leg with your arms and torso, grabbing your lower leg for support. Use your arms to pull your body down toward your leg. When grabbing the support leg, be sure to reach for the calf muscle. Keep your forehead facing the leg so that you don't strain your neck. Hold this position for 20 seconds, then repeat the exercise on the opposite side of your body.

Head to knee

COOLING DOWN

It's almost as important to cool down properly as it is to warm up. At the end of any practice, whether it covers forms, silk reeling, standing, or push hands, the breathing sequence is an excellent closing exercise.

CIRCLE ARMS OUTSIDE IN

Stand with your feet together and your arms at your sides. Raise your arms up and over your head slowly in a large circular motion.

Inhale deeply from your diaphragm as your arms rise. Now, place your palms together over your head and lower your hands down in front of your body with the palms together. As your palms pass your waist, allow them to separate and move next to your legs, with your palms facing your outer thighs. Repeat this twice.

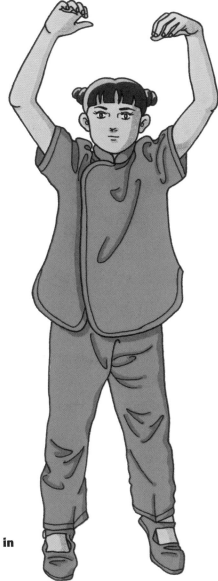

Circle arms outside in

CIRCLE ARMS INSIDE OUT

Continue from the first posture, standing with your feet together and arms at the sides of the body. Allow your palms to come together forming a cup under your navel, as if

Circle arms inside out

you're cupping water in the center of your hands. Slowly raise your arms up and over your head.

Inhale deeply from your diaphragm as you raise your arms. Now release your palms over your head and lower your hands down to the sides of your body with the palms gently going down, ending by your legs with your palms facing your thighs.

CIRCLE ARMS OUTSIDE FRONT

Continue from the second posture described above. With your feet together and your arms at the sides of your body, allow your palms to come together forming a cup under your navel, as if you're cupping water in the center of your hands. Gently raise your arms forward and upward to your chest. Gently turn the palms of your hands inward so that they face you. Open your palms over your head and lower your hands down to the sides of your body. Your palms should move gently down to the sides of your legs with your palms facing your thighs.

Next, inhale deeply from your diaphragm and raise your arms again. Turn your palms over so that they face the ground as your hands gently descend down past your waist and to the sides of your body.

Circle arms outside front

five
STANCES

Once you've warmed up, you'll start to practice your stances. Perfecting these stances will give you the strength and coordination you need to progress in Tai Chi. For example, we recommend practicing the stances in this chapter before trying the silk reeling exercises.

BASIC BODY MOVEMENTS

Tai Chi stances are made up of several subtle body movements. Let's get started by discussing some of these essential elements.

Stepping

It's important to remember to step with your heel first when moving forward and to step your toe first when moving backward. When stepping to the side, step with your heel first and pivot your foot until both toes face generally forward. You should feel very solid and stable in these stances. As you step, don't try to move too fast. Allow your weight to transfer only after you have secured your step.

Arm Movements

Your arms should always be relaxed so that you can move from one position to another with ease. As you move your arms, be sure that you're coordinating your upper body with your lower. Be alert for tension in your shoulders, and relax them by slowly dropping your elbows.

Leg Movements

Your legs should always feel comfortable with the direction they are bending in. If something feels unnatural as your legs move from one place to another, adjust your position until the move feels right, and then continue. Test your leg strength by extending and retracting your legs in different stances in the forms or silk reeling exercises.

Head Position

Your head controls the direction of your body, so watch its position. Looking down, for example, can throw you off-balance. Keep your head up. It's good for your alignment and general balance. Use the bean bag games that follow to develop good posture and body alignment.

Key parts of the body in Tai Chi movement

Waist ⇨ controls

Eyes ⇨ direct

Hands ⇨ follow

Hips and Groin

Your hips and groin usually open (your legs spread apart) as you bend your knees and sink (lower) your body. Try placing your fingers on your hips as you bend at the waist to feel your hips sinking. As you get more experienced, you'll feel that the movements come not from the knees, but actually from the hip sinking and groin opening, as if you were sitting on a chair. Note that when you're moving, your groin usually opens, and when you are settling into a posture, it closes.

Knees

As you bend your knees, be sure they do not pass the front of your toes. If you bend your knees too far, your body will feel strained. This is your body talking to you—saying that you have gone too far! Adjust your feet if you have trouble moving the leg that is not bearing your weight. Your knees should bend naturally and comfortably.

Hands

The hands play a very special part in Tai Chi movements. They guide the body, showing it where to go. Think of your hands as engines of a train, pulling your body along. As you use your hands to guide and pull your body through their motions, be sure to keep all of the cars connected. Your hands should always be relaxed and soft.

Eyes

Your eyes also play a key role in Tai Chi training. They direct your body where to go and how fast. They should always be alert and sharp. As you move your hands, your eyes should follow your movement attentively, always remaining coordinated with the speed and direction of your movements.

STANCES

Proper stances are largely responsible for the power for which Tai Chi is famous. This is especially true if you practice your stances diligently early in your training.

When performing all the stances, be sure that your hips are open and your feet are flat—as if you were grabbing the ground with your feet. In the single-leg stance be sure that your support leg is always slightly bent. You should always feel as if you can move easily from one stance to another. If this is difficult, it might mean that you have stepped too widely and should take a narrower stance.

FRONT TO BACK STANCES

With your hands on your waist, transfer your weight from your right leg to your left leg. Pivot your right foot slightly forward as you transfer your weight to your left leg. Your back leg should be directly behind your right shoulder. Keep your weight on your right leg and hold this posture for 30 seconds. After 30 seconds simply shift your weight to your right leg and hold for 30 seconds.

Front to back stances

Side to side stances

SIDE TO SIDE STANCES

With your hands still on your waist, transfer your weight to the right leg and step to the left side of the body. Keep your weight on the right leg while holding this posture. With your hands still on your waist, transfer your weight from the right leg to the left leg. Keep your weight on the left using the same weight distribution as in the other previous side stance posture. Also hold this posture for 30 seconds.

Next bend both legs as if you're sitting on a stool with most of the weight on the right leg. Keep the weight on the right leg and hold this posture for 30 seconds. Repeat.

ZHANG ZHUANG

Zhang zhuang, or the basic standing exercise, is one of the first things taught in Tai Chi. It requires a great amount of focus, concentration, and patience to execute properly. When done correctly, zhang zhuang practice produces a steady focus, while building internal strength and proper body alignment.

ZHANG ZHUANG REQUIREMENTS AND TECHNIQUE

■ Stand with your head erect, feet shoulders' width apart, legs slightly bent, and arms reaching out with bent elbows, just

Zhang zhuang

While standing in the zhang zhuang position, focus on an object, any object, about 10 feet in front of you and at eye level. Use that object as a focal point to concentrate on.

below chest height, as if gently hugging someone.

■ Touch the roof of your mouth with your tongue, while keeping your mouth gently closed.

■ Do not allow your weight to rest too much on your heels or the balls of your feet. Keep your ankles straight, maintaining an even distribution of weight on your feet.

■ Relax your chest and shoulders, allowing your elbows to drop slightly, with your palms facing your chest.

Let your knees bend in response to the relaxation of your hips and waist. However, it is very important that you not let your knees bend too far forward past your toes, but rather keep them over the middle of your foot, just in front of your ankle. Your thigh muscles should be engaged throughout the exercise. Try to feel your spine suspended and open, allowing its natural curves to manifest themselves. Your shoulder blades will gradually curve away from your spine as you sink into the posture. It is common for the body to move by itself as the muscles relax. Come out of this posture slowly, letting your hands sink down and your legs slowly straighten. Savor the peaceful sense of grounding and absorb the energy it creates.

The goal in practicing zhang zhuang is not to hold the posture for as long as possible. Instead, you should begin with a 5-minute pose. Add 1 minute every week, up to a maximum of 20 minutes for beginners.

GAMES WITH ZHANG ZHUANG

You can use beanbags as a fun training tool that helps you pay close attention to the proper postures that are crucial in Tai Chi. The beanbag becomes an extension of your body that must stay "connected" as you move through proper positions. If your body is in the wrong position, the bag will let you know by falling off your head!

BEANBAG ON HEAD

Starting from the zhang zhuang position, place a small beanbag on top of your head. Try to keep it in place for 1 minute without dropping the bag. As you improve, you can add more time to this exercise.

BEANBAGS ON HANDS

While standing in the zhang zhuang position, place one beanbag on the back of each hand, resting the beanbag on top of your thumb and first finger (index finger). Your hands should be positioned as if you are holding a cup—imagine how a cup would fit into the shape of your hand. Try to keep your arms extended while maintaining a slight bend in your elbows. Hold this position for 1 minute without dropping the beanbags. As you improve, you can add more time to this exercise. Pay attention to your shoulder tension. Be sure to relax your shoulders so that they are not shrugging upward. Also, as noted, focus on an object at eye level that's about 10 feet in front of you.

STANCE SEQUENCE

This routine will help you understand how the stances blend together into basic sequences of movement. This sequence

should be practiced slowly with emphasis on precise movements and proper alignment. Tai Chi teachers often use yin and yang to represent different sides of the body—yang indicates the weight-bearing side of the body, while yin indicates the opposite or non-weight-bearing side.

Stance sequence step 1

1. Pivot your right foot.

2. Step forward with your left foot and "sit" into a back stance. (See the description of the back stance on page 21.)

3. Transfer your weight forward onto your left leg so that you end up in a front stance.

4. Bring your right leg forward, placing the ball of your foot slightly ahead of your left foot. Make sure that your right leg is directly in front of your right shoulder and not in front of your left foot.

Stance sequence step 6

Stance sequence step 5

Stance sequence step 7

5. Raise your right knee up to waist height, balancing on your left leg.

6. Place your right heel down on the floor in front of your right shoulder.

7. Turn your torso to the right, making sure that your shoulders and hips are facing in the same direction. Bend your knees into a cross-legged sitting position.

8. From the sitting position step out to the left side of your body with your left foot, keeping your weight on your right leg.

Stance sequence step 8

Stance sequence step 10

9. Transfer your weight to your left leg very slowly.

10. Step with your right leg behind your left leg and turn to the right. Make a half turn so that your body faces the opposite direction.

11. Step back with your left leg as you extend both hands forward, with your palms facing up.

Stance sequence step 11

12. Step back with your right leg as you bring your hands back to your waist, standing with your feet together.

Stance sequence step 12

In all Tai Chi movements, stay loose and. don't hold any tension in your body. The guided imagery exercise[s] on page 41 can help.

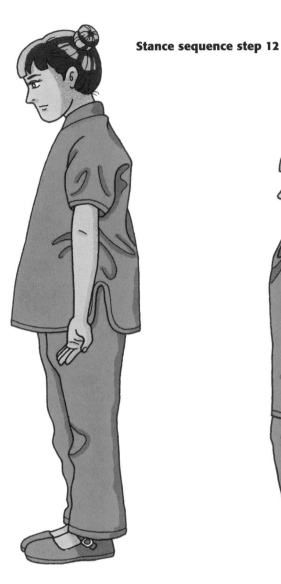

Stance sequence step 13a

27

13. Circle your arms up to your sides, then down, until they reach each side of your body.

14. Repeat the sequence in reverse, to train the opposite side of your body.

Stance sequence step 13b

The practice of Tai Chi is built around sequences of repeated movements. The body builds a physical memory of these movements as you practice them. As you improve, you will be able to sense when your body moves perfectly and when it is "off." This is one physical benefit of learning Tai Chi—knowing when your body is connected and when it is not. Once you can feel and tell the difference, you are well on your way to understanding the true nature and value of Tai Chi.

Picturing your body as a tree is an effective way to practice stances. Imagine that your feet are the roots, your legs and torso are the trunk of the tree, your arms and head branches, and finally your fingertips are the leaves. When wind hits a tree, it absorbs the wind in its leaves by swaying left or right, deflecting strong winds and usually surviving storms. The more the wind blows, the more power the tree stores. This is true of Tai Chi as well: the more you practice, the stronger you get.

- Remember to step with your heel first when moving forward and with your toe first when moving backward.

- Keep your arms relaxed so that you can move from one position to another with ease.

- Remember that your legs should always feel comfortable with the direction they are bending in.

- Keep your head up.

- Keep your hands on your hips and feel your hips sinking when you bend.

- Remember that your knees should bend naturally and comfortably.

- Remember that your hands guide the body.

- Keep your eyes alert and sharp.

Six

PRACTICING TAI CHI

After building a foundation with stances, your training will progress to silk reeling exercises. These help develop the connection between the leg strength developed during stance training and whole-body movements.

SILK REELING

In silk reeling the idea is to connect all parts of your body, leading with your waist as you move your weight from one part of the body to another. Think of your upper and lower body as two bottles—one full of water, the other empty. As you fill the empty bottle (upper body) with water (transfer your weight), the water needs time to pour into the other bottle. Your job is to use your waist to balance this pouring and avoid any breaks in your movement. When the full bottle (lower body) pours its water completely into the empty bottle (upper body), your waist will have transferred your energy from your lower to your upper body as you move. This image also describes the transfer of weight and energy from the left to right sides of your body.

SINGLE-ARM SILK REELING

1. Place your left hand on your left hip as you sink your weight onto your left foot.

Single-arm silk reeling step 1

As you sink, raise your right arm so that your palm is facing up with your fingers pointing away from your body to the left corner. Now, step out to the right side of your body, with your feet wider than shoulders' width apart. Keep your weight on your left leg.

2. Next, start to "wipe" your right arm to your right as you transfer your weight to the right

Double-arm silk reeling step 1

Single-arm silk reeling step 2

side of your body. Continue the circle until you come back to the right side of your body once again. Now switch your arms by placing your right hand on your right waist and extending your left hand so that it is in front of your right shoulder. Repeat the same circular movement on the left side of your body.

DOUBLE-ARM SILK REELING

1. Starting with your feet together, pivot your right foot to your right, then shift your weight to your right leg. Now, step to your left with your left leg, with your left heel touching the floor behind your left ear. Gently bring your arms out to the right

Double-arm silk reeling step 2

side of the body as if pushing to the right. Your arms should be chest high.

2. With your weight on your right leg, side wipe both arms to your left. As they pass your right hip, start to transfer your weight to your left leg, guiding your hands in front of your body so that they glide from right to left.

Double-arm silk reeling step 3b

Double-arm silk reeling step 3a

3. Now gently glide your hands back and continue to circle them back to your original position. To move to the other side of your body, simply pivot your left foot to your left while your weight is on your right foot, and continue with another wipe.

The essence of Tai Chi practice is the development of chan szu jing (silk reeling energy). Both in theory and in practice, chan szu jing can be considered a tool for refining your Tai Chi movements. As you work at developing the qualities of chan szu jing, remember that your goal is to build efficient movement, directed by your waist and powered by your legs.

PUSH HANDS

Push hands (tui shou) is one of the best examples of the concept of yin and yang in action. It is, in fact, a physical manifestation of yin and yang.

When you practice push hands be sure to pay attention to the direction of your internal energy. Try to imagine where you are sending your force as you circle your arm. Be sure to coordinate the movement of your limbs with your waist, connecting your whole body to the movement. In partner push hands try to feel the direction of your opponent's force. Also try to stay aware of the constant shifting of your weight during pushing and absorbing movements.

Single-arm push hands

SINGLE-ARM PUSH HANDS

Stand with your feet together and your arms gently at your sides. Shift your weight to your left leg, pivot your right foot out, and then transfer your weight back to your right leg. Next extend your left leg forward, stepping by placing your heel down first.

Your foot should be placed forward, diagonally and to the left. Now, extend your left arm out so that it is chest high, with your fingers facing up and your palm facing in. Your right hand is placed on your hip. Gently shift your weight from your right leg to your left leg as you circle your extended hand horizontally. Continue to circle your arm by bending your elbow as you transfer

your weight back, and extending it as you go forward. Repeat this five times.

Then, switch to the other side of your body by pivoting your left foot out, transferring your weight onto that leg, and stepping forward with your right foot. Be sure that your right leg is not directly in front of your left leg. It should be to the right, just outside your left heel in a forward diagonal position. Repeat this five to ten times. To finish, simply step back, bringing your leg back to your original standing position. Place your arms at your sides. Remember: when you extend your arm, your palm should face forward. When you pull your arm back, your palm should face your chest.

DOUBLE-ARM PUSH HANDS

Start as in the previous exercise, but sweep both your arms across your torso at chest height. Your right leg should move forward at the same time that you sweep your arms across your body. Your arms should move simultaneously, in the same position. It should feel as if you're moving just one arm.

PUSH HANDS WITH A PARTNER

This exercise is the highlight of Tai Chi. When you do it, you learn about the absorption and redirection of qi. Your emphasis should not be on who can push the hardest—but on who can neutralize or counter their partner the best. It can also be played as a sort of game, by assigning each of you a role as either yin (absorbing) or yang (pushing).

DOUBLE-PALM PUSH

While facing your partner, push both of your palms against the palms of the other person, standing with your feet shoulders' width apart. This game teaches you the principles of absorbing incoming forces. The goal is to avoid falling off-balance, while sinking your hips. It's fun to try to regain your balance. You can even keep score by awarding points to the one whose feet stay in their original place.

Double-palm push and strike

DOUBLE-PALM STRIKE

While facing each other and using the same positioning as in the double-palm push, strike both of your palms against your partner's as you stand with your feet shoulders' width apart. This is a variation on the first game, but requires a different approach to absorbing the incoming force. The goal again is to sink to retain your balance.

PUSH HANDS WITH BALL

Using a ball in Tai Chi games can help you develop manipulation skills. This is another great example of seeing yin/yang in action within your Tai Chi practice.

This game can be played with any ball the size of a volleyball or basketball. Start by facing your partner, arm's length apart with your feet shoulders' width apart. Next, step forward with your right foot, and extend your right palm. The ball is placed between

Side pulling

SIDE PULLING

With you and your partner facing in opposite directions, stand in a wide stance, holding each other's left hand at your left sides. Once in the stance, try to upset your partner's balance by pushing forward or pulling back. If your partner loses his or her balance, switch sides (hands) and try again.

Push hands with ball

In push hands, your elbows should stay near your hips.

your hand and your partner's hand.

Now, begin circling the ball in all possible directions without losing control. Push it back and forth and up and down until someone loses contact with the ball and it drops. Each pair can be a team—and the team who keeps the ball "in play" the longest is the winner.

Another variation would be to use only your inner wrist while trying to maintain contact with the ball. This variation is much more difficult, so you should start with the palm version.

A third version involves using only your forearms to rotate the ball without dropping it.

Still another variation of this game is to toss the ball using just your forearms. Your partner then has to catch the ball using only his or her forearms. In this variation, you and your partner should stand about 6 feet apart. Increase the distance as you get more accurate in the game.

For even more fun, develop yin and yang teams. When you notice one team getting better at their role than the other, switch roles.

SPARRING

Tai Chi is usually considered a "moving meditation," but it has its roots in martial arts, and advanced practitioners study sparring techniques.

Sparring practice usually starts from the base of tui shou. Traditionally, once you have perfected five increasingly sophisticated levels of push hands, you'll begin to practice sparring. Live sparring usually begins out of the free-stepping learned in push hands training, which is usually introduced at the intermediate level. Fundamental (Chen style) Tai Chi sparring is akin to upright wrestling. It then progresses to close-quarters striking before moving toward advanced combat practice with an emphasis on body and joint locking.

You'll need to practice Tai Chi for a while before you start training in sparring, but the pushing and pulling exercises in this chapter are an important part of the necessary skills.

35

Tai Chi helps you get your mind and body working as one. You'll have:

- Better breathing from practicing deep breathing

- Better balance from working on your motor skills

- Better emotional health from the peace and serenity that comes from the slow, measured movements

- Heightened senses from the focused concentration you apply to your practice

- Better pain management from better body alignment and deep breathing

seven

CONDITIONING

To succeed in Tai Chi, it's essential to practice. However, along with practicing the movements and postures, it's important to develop your mind and body. The following conditioning exercises will help you strengthen your body and focus your mind.

PHYSICAL CONDITIONING

Tai Chi has unique physical requirements, so most teachers include strength and conditioning exercises in their classes. These exercises will help you develop a combination of balance and strength. They are crucial for strengthening your legs, which are a very important part of Tai Chi. The following exercises address different body parts. Legs, arms, and abdominal strength are all important.

Standing single-leg balance

STANDING SINGLE-LEG BALANCE

Start with your feet shoulders' width apart. Transfer your weight to your right leg, and slowly bring your left knee toward your chest. Grab your knee with your left hand and your ankle with your right hand. Pull your leg as close to your body as you can. Try to hold this position for 30 seconds. Slowly lower your leg to the shoulders' width position. Repeat with the opposite leg.

TAI CHI SQUATS: SOLO

While standing in the zhang zhuang position (see page 22), try to slowly lower your body to a full squat position while maintaining erect posture. Your hands should be extended in front of you as if you're standing in the basic zhang zhuang position. Give yourself 20 seconds to squat and 20 seconds to stand back up. For fun, you can try this with a beanbag on your head. The objective is to keep your head straight and not drop the beanbag.

Solo Squats

TAI CHI SQUATS: WITH A PARTNER

Sit facing your partner and place your feet together so that your toes are touching. Reach across and grab each other's wrists firmly. Once you both have a firm grip, try to stand slowly at the same time. When you both reach a full standing position, try to lower yourselves back to the sitting position without making a sound. This exercise should also be done with a 20-second count.

Partner squats

WALKING PUSH-UPS: SOLO

Stand with your feet together. Squat down
to a full squatting position, placing your
hands on the floor in front of you.
"Walk" forward on your hands to a
fully stretched out position (like a
push-up position). Lower your body
until your chest touches the floor
once. Push your body back off the
floor, then "walk" back to your original squat position. Stand back up.
Repeat the exercise. This time with
two push-ups, then stand. Add an
extra push-up for every walk-out
you do.

Walking push-ups: solo 1

This exercise not only builds your upper
body strength, but also helps you learn
about weight distribution
as you constantly shift your
weight from one arm to the
other. You can feel yin and
yang working together
while practicing this
exercise.

Walking push-ups: solo 2

WALKING PUSH-UPS: WITH A PARTNER

Start from a lying down position—on your stomach with your hands near the sides of your chest. Your partner should also be on the ground in front of you, with the top of his head facing the top of yours. Push up until your arms are fully extended, then walk back to a squat position. Stand up slowly.

Next, squat down to a full squatting position placing your hands on the floor in front of you. Walk out to a fully stretched out position (the push-up position) and do one push-up. You and your partner should try to do each of these steps at the same time. Once you're both in the full push-up position, try to lift your right hand off the ground, and give your partner's right hand a quick slap. Lower yourself to the floor, walk with your hands back into the original squatting position, then stand. Repeat with your partner, adding an extra push-up for every walk-out you do.

Walking push-ups: with a partner

Tri-ups

TRI-UPS

Lie on your back, and extend your arms directly over your head. Raise your right knee up to your right shoulder as you bring your upper body up to meet your knee. Lie back down, then come up again, this time with your left knee to your left shoulder. The third time raise both knees to meet both shoulders, then lie back down. This counts as one tri-up. Try to do five. On the fifth one, try to balance on your buttocks, holding your legs

Tri-ups Variation

For fun, gently pound on your stomach, like Tarzan or King Kong, before returning from the balance position to the lying down position.

out with your hands reaching in front of your body. Count to five, then lie back down with your arms on the floor extended back over your head. This exercise builds strength in both the upper and lower abdominal muscles. Again, you can also physically feel the yin and yang of this exercise.

MENTAL CONDITIONING: MEDITATION

Meditation is quite difficult, even for adults, especially still meditation (meditation without movement). The following meditation activities will help you focus your mind. These activities are designed both to build a mind-body connection—very important in Tai Chi—and to help you explore your imagination.

GUIDED IMAGERY

While standing in the zhang zhuang position, close your eyes and take an imaginary trip though your body. The key phrase here is *"relax my. . . ."* Start by thinking "relax my. . . ." Complete the thought with the name of a specific body part. Focus your thoughts on the body part you just named. Start from your feet, then work up to your knees, then your hips, toward your arms, shoulders, elbows, wrists, and fingers, back to your neck,

Guided imagery

then to the top of your head. Finally, just listen—focus on the sounds of wherever you are—the park, a classroom, and so on. As you listen, start taking the same trip through your body, this time backward, until you finally get all the way back to your feet. Once there, slowly open your eyes. Your trip is complete. Be sure to come out of your posture *very* slowly.

As an alternative: Imagine that as you breathe in your breath is going to a specific part of your body. Then as you breathe out any tension in that area is carried out of you as you exhale. Start with your feet and work your way up to the top of your head.

COUNTING

Sometimes it's difficult to concentrate or focus on clearing your mind in meditation. So, instead of clearing it, why not fill it? This method will help you focus on something specific. It can be done sitting on a chair with your back upright or in the zhang zhuang position. To start, imagine a screen showing an image inside your forehead. Start with the image of the number 1, flashing in your head for one second. Follow this with the image of the number 2. Count—image by image, number by number—up to number 10. Once you hit 10, start your count again—from the number 1. Breathing is important, so try to coordinate your breaths—your inhalations and exhalations—with each count. Keep your tongue against the roof of your mouth while doing this.

eight

ADVANCING IN TAI CHI

Advancing in Tai Chi takes dedication and a positive attitude. It also takes a well-rounded approach to the art. For example, if you focus on just the positions, you'll probably lose some of the mental focus that complements the physical movements.

Here are five main keys to remember for your Tai Chi practice. Follow these guidelines and you're sure to go far in Tai Chi.

THE FIVE KEYS TO ADVANCING IN TAI CHI

Practice

As with all things in life, if you want to become good at something, you have to practice. A good method is to take a newly learned form or movement and repeat it ten times in a row, doing it slower and slower each time. Part of the power of Tai Chi comes from moving slowly so that your muscles can move very fast when you need to. But it also helps build up a physi-

cal memory, allowing your body to store the movement into its memory banks.

Breathing

During practice you should try to connect your breathing to the movement. This takes a lot of concentration and timing. So, don't be discouraged if you don't get it at first. It requires you to pay attention to when your body is moving and when it is stopping. You should place your tongue on the roof of your mouth and press your lips together gently. Your breathing should be deep and go in and out through your nostrils. As you breathe pay attention to the rising and settling of your stomach. Overall, when pushing or exerting, exhale. When pulling or relaxing, inhale.

Repetition

The purpose of repetition is not to simply repeat movement but to improve on every attempt the sequence being practiced. Each attempt gradually improves on the previous one. The trick is to pay attention to how much better each one feels and looks. Always remember that practice does not make perfect—perfect practice makes perfect.

Focus

Always be aware of details such as balance and connection. When you really focus on the details of what you are doing, your Tai Chi becomes more clear and precise. Try not to let your mind wander. It's very easy to get caught up in the form after you know a routine. The hard part is to keep focused on your feet and hands moving as one. This is the goal for all practitioners of Tai Chi.

Understanding

Think about what you're doing as you do it. Be like a scientist trying to figure out why something works. As you practice slowly you'll find that many things you never noticed start to appear. It's only when you understand the how and why that you'll really appreciate what you just learned.

THE FIVE LEVELS OF TAI CHI

Studying Tai Chi is like going from elementary school through to college. The process of acquiring knowledge is a gradual one. Without the fundamental knowledge acquired in elementary school and high school, the student cannot absorb the lessons taught in college. Learning Tai Chi is the same. New knowledge and understanding is built on what is acquired in previous stages. If you violate this principle and attempt to jump ahead prematurely, you will only lengthen your learning process.

Even though traditional Chinese martial arts don't use a belt system, as in Karate, there are well-defined, clear-cut stages of progression that students must pass through.

Chen Tai Chi specifically has five skill levels that are pursued by the long-term student. Summarized below, the first four levels distill classic (Chen style) Tai Chi principles applicable to all Tai Chi styles.* There are objective standards and criteria for each of these levels. The following section introduces the technical skills achieved at each of these levels. This should help you assess your current level and know what areas you need to work on to advance to the next level.

Level 1: Form and Posture

In the beginning, your body is not well connected. As you develop strength through good postures, you will see less angular and disconnected movement. The stance practices and games will help you in this area of development, since leg strength is crucial at this stage of your training. Over time you'll experience improvement in the direction and position of your movement and limbs, while achieving correct postures.

Level 2: Body and Mind Synthesis

Here, you'll have to be more mindful of your practice by carefully watching your body's movement. Thinking of where your weight is and concentrating on slow movements are good ways to get your mind and body to work as one. At this stage you'll understand your movements better, and your body will begin to make sense of what is happening during practice. You should be able to fine-

43

*Howard Choy and Ahtee Chia, "Family Transmitted Chen Style Tai Chi Chuan" *Inside Kung Fu*, May 1992, pp. 41–43, 80.

tune your postures and understand how to express power and speed and control. Because you are stronger, you may begin to challenge yourself through some of the games in your training. You should begin to feel comfortable correcting yourself at this point.

Level 3: Thinking of Circles

At this level you should think of all the movements you've been practicing as circles—some big, some small. As you get better, these circles get smaller until no one can see them, but you can feel them. At this advanced level, you'll move from thinking about big circles to thinking about small circles. Your movements should be continuous and without weakness in any part of your body. Your movements should be sure and natural.

Level 4: Qi Flow

At this stage you will begin to feel an intrinsic heat not fueled by strenuous exercise. This internal energy is known as qi. As your movements smooth out and your postures steady, you'll begin to sense an internal warmth, especially in your hands. At this stage you should focus on relaxing your

body, by hollowing your chest and slightly tucking your buttocks in, while keeping your spine straight. These more subtle physical movements will enhance the flow of qi and your sensation of it.

Level 5: Balancing Hard and Soft

As you progress through the first four levels, your movements will soften, but not be limp. Your Tai Chi will resemble a balance of hard and soft, fast and slow, bent and straight. When you're able to move while balancing different types of energy in your body, you Tai Chi will exhibit a balance of forces—a balance of yin and yang.

CONCLUSION

To advance in Tai Chi, adhere to the principles of yin and yang in your practice. Whenever you notice the physical changes that will occur in your Tai Chi, you'll know that you're ready for the next stage. Understanding the five levels of Tai Chi will help guide your practice and provide you with hints that will signal when you are able to progress to higher levels.

ACKNOWLEDGMENTS

Jose Figueroa would like to thank the following people for their contributions that made this book possible.

Models:
Natalie Figueroa
Cheikh Fall

Hair and make up:
Awilda & Nadia Figueroa
Natasha Bolado

Photography & layout:
Johnny Rodriquez (jrvisions.com)

The following places and people opened their hearts and minds to the idea of Tai Chi for kids and the value of such a program.

P.S. 121 / Scan New York
Lewis Zuckerman and Rene Avery, for being amazing mentors in the development and growth of our youth.

P.S./M.S. 20
Rita Sollow Schneyman and staff of P.S./M.S. 20 in the Bronx, for believing that the gift of Tai Chi enhances the academic and social performance of children. And to all of the children who taught me how to truly teach from the heart.

Manhattan School for Children
Susan Rappaport, Alysa Essenfeld, and Anna Chen, as well as the magnificent staff, parents, and kids that made this program such a success and joy, Thank you all for helping refine this unique curriculum.

A SPECIAL THANKS goes out to all of my mentors and teachers. Thank you, Master Derrick Trent, my first Tai Chi teacher, for introducing me to the legacy that is Tai Chi. To Master Ren Guang Yi for his powerful inspiration, guidance, and support on the development of this complex art. And thanks to my kung fu brothers Greg Pinney and the late Dr. Joseph Cheu for your knowledge and mutual love for Tai Chi.

AND A VERY SPECIAL THANKS goes to Stephan Berwick, who has inspired me to achieve goals that I never thought possible. This book could not have been done without your guidance, support and deep expertise in the martial arts. You represent the highest qualities of a Martial Artist. Both warrior and scholar, you do it from the heart, not for fame or money, but for the love of Kung Fu and the splendor it brings. Many of my lessons with you were much more about the true meaning of Kung Fu and what it truly represents to the practitioner. In your voice I can hear the passion and love for the art. Your lessons to me were much more about inspiration than anything else. What stays with me is your ability to be so humble about your development in the martial arts. For this reason I'm proud to have you as my co-writer, mentor and life friend. You are a modern Shih Fu who refrains from the title Master, but is truly worthy of it.

ABOUT THE AUTHORS

JOSE FIGUEROA

Jose Figueroa's more than fifteen years in Chinese martial arts includes unrivaled success as America's premier internal Chinese martial arts competitor. Founder of the Tai Chi Holistic Network, Mr. Figueroa is a senior student of Master Ren Guang Yi. He has won numerous grand championships and first place titles at every major Chinese martial arts tournament in the United States. As a national champion, he traveled to China in 1998 with Master Ren to train in Chen village and compete in the International Taiji Competition held in Wenxian, Henan, China.

With a BS in Physical Education, Mr. Figueroa has designed innovative physical education curricula based solely on Chinese martial arts for the NY Board of Education, Wavehill community, Equinox health club, and the Omega Institute. From 1996-2004, under mentoring by Mr. Berwick, Mr. Figueroa emerged as one of New York's favored theater choreographers. For his pioneering work with jazz playwright Fred Ho, Mr. Figueroa won the 2000 NY Foundation for the Arts Gregory Millard fellowship for choreography, based on his use of Chinese martial arts for theater combat choreography.

STEPHAN BERWICK

Stephan Berwick, a winner of the 1st International Chen Style Taijiquan Association Excellence Award, has almost 30 years experience in Chinese martial arts. A widely published martial arts scholar and practitioner, Stephan is a senior disciple of Master Ren Guang Yi and is also trained by Grandmaster Chen Xiaowang. Certified at the Sha'anxi Athletic Technical Institute in Xi'an China, under Masters Zhao Changjun and Bai Wenxiang, Stephan later conducted primary research on Chen Taijiquan at Taiji's birthplace, Chenjiagou.

Stephan was originally mentored by **Master Bow Sim Mark** and performed in Hong Kong action films with **Donnie Yen** under director **Yuen Wo Ping**. As a Chen Taiji specialist, Stephan instructs a wide variety of students — from the physically challenged to experienced defense professionals. For more information on Stephan's Washington DC-area Taiji program, please visit http://www.truetaichi.com.

OTHER BOOKS IN THIS SERIES

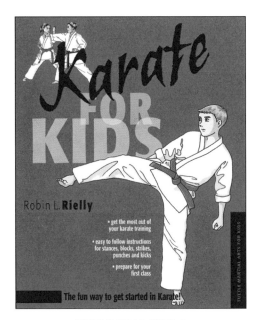

ISBN 0-8048-3534-9

ISBN 0-8048-3600-0

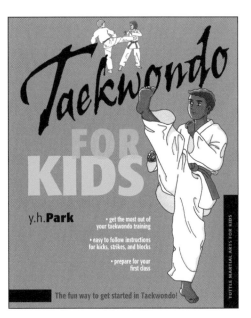

ISBN 0-8048-3631-0